The Little Book of Personal Development, Success and Happiness

Hannu Pirilä

The Little Book of Personal Development, Success and Happiness

Useful thoughts to get insights and ideas for a better
and happier life

Second edition

Illustrations: Hannu Pirilä
Editing: Hannu Pirilä

Publisher: BoD™ – Books on Demand, Helsinki, Suomi
Printer: Books on Demand GmbH, Norderstedt, Germany
ISBN: 9789528023166

Index

Foreword

It is an honor to get to write a foreword to Hannu Pirilä's first book.

I have known Hannu for more than ten years now. Hannu has worked as a Consultant and Mentor for my business and as a Mental Coach in my preparation for different martial arts fights. During the years we have become good friends and business partners. We have also sat long nights together and "improved the world," as we tend to say in Finland.

I have always been fascinated by Hannu's desire to help people to do more of those things that are important to them. I have also witnessed how Hannu has himself taken some brave steps in his life, abandoning a well-paid job to become an entrepreneur and leaving the field of hotel consulting, that he mastered so well, to the background.

Hannu is doing those things in his life that he feels are important and that he really believes in. In our numerous conversations I have been impressed by how Hannu particularly wants to help individual persons and smaller companies to achieve goals that are important to them.

I have read Hannu's book several times and I am happy to notice that its content genuinely looks like the way he is. I hope that everyone who gets this book in their hands, reads it with an open mind and that they find those keys to success and happiness – and that they also take them into good use.

I want to congratulate Hannu for this close-knit book on personal development, success and happiness. Furthermore, I respect the fact that he has taken the time between all other work to write it.

May this book bring us all clarity and light as we steer our lives toward our future goals and great adventures!"

Helsinki, 3rd of January 2013

Timo Räkköläinen
Helsingin Itsepuolustuskoulu Oy, Hipko (Helsinki Self-Defense School Ltd)
CEO, Founder and Head Instructor

Introduction

I had my first touch on personal development almost two decades ago, when my girlfriend at that time introduced me to books like The Seven Habits of Highly Effective People by Stephen R. Covey, The Road Less Traveled by M. Scott Peck and The Celestine Prophecy by James Redfield.

Since then, my interest toward personal development and spirituality has gradually increased to what it is today, which is my profession.

Today, personal development and spirituality to me mean to continuously study and develop myself in different areas of life. My studies include certifications like executive Master of Business Administration, Licensed Master Practitioner and Trainer of NLP™, Licensed NLP Coach™, Licensed Master Business NLP™ Practitioner, Licensed LAB Profile™ Practitioner and Licensed Sports Performance Coach™.

As a sort of a byproduct of my self-development process, I have gained huge amounts of knowledge and skills that I can use to help other people, as well. Therefore, I am nowadays a professional consultant, coach and trainer helping businesses and individuals to achieve the results they want. Oftentimes, this also means achieving success and happiness.

One of the ways I offer my help to people is to write articles and blogs on things I come across in my work. This way I can give some pieces of advice to people who are seeking that kind of information. And it also helps me, because putting my thoughts down in writing is a great way for me to get some clarity of my thoughts.

This little book is really based on some of my articles that can be found in different places on the internet and that I have somewhat modified and perhaps updated for this book. In this book I have tried to put together some of the most important or helpful thoughts that I hope will help you as a reader to get some new insights and ideas on how to make your life at least a little bit better and happier – no matter how good or bad, happy or sad your life is at the moment. So, if you will get even one insight or idea that will improve your life, one way or another, writing this book has proven to be worth the effort.

Since I wanted to make this book as comprehensible and easy to read as possible, I have tried to express my thoughts as compressed as possible. On one hand this means that many of the subjects are left without in-depth explanations or pondering, but on the other hand, it leaves room for you as a reader to form your own opinions on things and also gives you ideas and inspiration to go out and explore your own route on your self-development.

The point, however, is that you will not get the whole picture of what personal development really means by just reading a book or taking a course on the subject. Personal development is a lifelong journey that requires constant studying and being open to new ideas and perceptions. I have read countless number of books and studied dozens of courses and programs, and from every book, course, program or seminar I always get something that deepens my knowledge and inspires me to be even better at what I love doing.

Therefore, if nothing else, I hope this book will give you a little nudge to dig in deeper to find out what you really want, what is your passion, and achieve the success and happiness that is out there waiting for you.

In January 2013

Hannu Pirilä

www.hannupirila.com

Introduction to the Second Edition

As I state in the Introduction of the first edition above, I think self-development should be continuous and life-long process. Thus, I have (at least in my opinion) evolved quite a bit during the seven years of the publication of the first edition of this book.

Along the way, I have read a large number of books, visited numerous seminars and completed, among other things, a Diploma in Clinical Hypnotherapist at International College of Clinical Hypnotherapy in London. I have also developed myself constantly in NLP (Neuro-linguistic programming), including attending regularly seminars of the developer of NLP, Dr. Richard Bandler, in a team of assistant trainers in London and Orlando.

In the meantime, I have also published a new book, *Your Own Blue Ocean*, which also contains an abundance of exercises and NLP techniques to help you make desired changes.

Since I have experienced more development myself over the years, I felt that it was time to upgrade this book a little bit. I have not made any major changes to the texts of the first edition, some minor updates, however. Instead, I have added to this second edition two new chapters that I have felt important to bring to this book. Although the number of pages in the book has increased slightly, it should still fit into the title of a little book.

I wish you inspiring moments with this second edition.

April, 2020

Hannu Pirilä

Why Do We Need Personal Development to Be Successful?

In order to be able to examine personal development as a part of our overall success in life, I feel it is necessary to define first what we mean by personal development. In my opinion, personal development is:

- Growth as a conscious human being
- Activities that improve self-knowledge and identity
- Development of talents and potential
- Development in different areas of life
- Building of human capital and employability
- Enhancing the quality of life
- Contributing to the realization of dreams and aspirations
- Is not limited to self-development but includes formal and informal activities for developing others
- In the context of institutions, it refers to the methods, programs, tools, techniques, and assessment systems that support human development at the individual level in organizations
- (Hard) Work that requires discipline, determination, consistency, patience, time, courage and forgiveness
- Increasing sensation of happiness

Let's then take a closer look at some of these bullet points in correlation to success.

Improving your self-knowledge and identity means, among other things, that you become more aware of who you are and what you want.

Knowing what you want and where you need to improve yourself in order to achieve what you want are essential parts of success.

If you have already achieved success you cannot stay put if you want to remain successful. The world and other people around you are constantly evolving; therefore, you need to keep on developing your talents and potential further. Otherwise your success will remain short term.

Depending on your goals, you need constant development in different areas of your life, not just in one. Some of these areas might include health, finances, relationships, emotions, habits and beliefs, to mention a few. A good health will ensure that you are able to do what you want to do. It is obvious that you can do a lot more as a healthy person than you would if lying sick on a bed. It is also obvious, in most cases, that you can achieve more and free yourself from many of the worries when your financial situation is stable. Furthermore, it is obvious that you can achieve more when you have sound relationships with supporting and loving people to back you up. And so on.

Having activities for developing others, in addition to developing yourself, is really what gives you the final boost for success. The old saying "what goes around, comes around" applies here quite well. Helping other people succeed will ensure that they willingly help you in return. It is much, much more difficult – and in most cases even impossible – to achieve success just by yourself. You can't be the master of everything. And you shouldn't even try to be. Concentrate on doing well what you love doing and let other people help you in the areas that they love doing. Help others develop themselves and they will help you develop yourself. That is for everybody's benefit.

> *"I think self-improvement is such a noble pursuit because it helps not only you but also the people around you, ultimately making the world a better place for all of us." -Paul McKenna*

Finally, understand that long lasting success does require work. At times, it can even seem to require hard work. But once you have found what it is that you truly love doing, the work doesn't seem that hard anymore. It will require discipline, though, so that you keep your focus on your goals. It will require determination because there will be a lot of people who'll try to talk you out of your dream. It will require consistency because you will encounter many obstacles along the way and you'll have to be consistent to work your way through and around them. It will require patience because the bigger your dream, the more it will take time to fulfill it. It will require courage because you will move toward something that is unknown to you. And, maybe most of all, it will require forgiveness because you will have to forgive yourself for all the mistakes you have made, and will make, and you must also forgive others who have hurt you, so you can move into the future with a clean slate.

And that is all part of the road to success.

"People who stop studying merely because they have finished school are forever hopelessly doomed to mediocrity, no matter what their calling. The way of success is the way of continuous pursuit of knowledge." - Napoleon Hill"

How to Find Authentic Happiness

I have studied success and happiness for many years now and I have come to find that those two go hand in hand in many ways. I think one of the best ways to describe success is by Deepak Chopra:

> *"Success in life could be defined as the continued expansion of happiness and the progressive realization of worthy goals… Moreover, success is a journey, not a destination."*

You see, *you* define what happiness is to *you*. What is it that makes you happy? One of the things that will make you happy is the progressive realization of your worthy goals. And you decide what goals are worthy of you.

You are constantly trading your life for something. Maybe it's your work. Are you trading 40 hours per week of your life for the money you get from your employer? If that work makes you happy, if you really love your work, then you're on the right track. The question to ask, though, is: "Is this work, and the money I earn from it, worthy of my time/life?"

So, the point is really: What is a goal that is worthy of you? What are you willing to trade your life for? When you find answers to those questions, you know what will make you happy.

Now notice that I said "you know what will make you happy" not "you will be happy." What will make you happy is the progressive realization of that worthy goal. In other words, that journey toward that worthy goal of yours.

So, that means that authentic and everlasting happiness is the ever growing feeling that comes from moving toward a goal that is worthy of you.

However, as always, you do have a choice:

In short: You can choose to be content, even happy, with what you got, and in a way you should, too. The thing is, though, that like Deepak Chopra, I believe that by constantly moving toward an even greater fulfillment in life, you will allow your happiness to grow.

I am aware that all that can be quite confusing and still leave you with several questions, like: "How do I find a goal that is worthy of me and my life?" or "How do I know if moving toward that goal will make me happy?"

Unfortunately, there are no unambiguous answers to those questions. I believe we all have our unique purpose in this world and that is for each and every one of us to find out. There are, however, techniques and ways that will help you find that out.

One of the ways is to start by writing down 30 things that you want to have, be or achieve. Just start scribbling them down. Then, when you've done that, what you need to do is to prioritize them. Really, put them into an order of importance from 1 to 30. When you have done that, take the Top 3 or 5 things from your list and write down why you want to have/achieve those things.

That exercise should give you some help and I recommend that you do it. However, by far the best techniques to find out what are the goals that are worthy of you and what will make you happy, are the techniques I have found in NLP (Neuro-Linguistic Programming).

With NLP you learn to set well-formed goals, or well-formed directions, which are a must in order for you to know which direction to go to. NLP also has several other excellent techniques and exercises, like the Logical Levels, which will help you by checking if what you are doing is in sync with your "higher self" and your purpose.

The only downside with those techniques and exercises is that they would take a lot of space to explain in this little book. Therefore, I recommend that you:

1. Read the chapter about goal setting (Five Tips for Setting Goals) in this book
2. Get some books on NLP and/or
3. Sign up for an NLP course.

The interesting thing is, like I pointed out at the beginning of this chapter, that several studies show that those people who consider themselves to be happy, consider themselves to be successful, too. The truth is that the happier you are, the more successful you are, as well. In the end, you define what success is to you.

(A brief introduction to NLP can be found at the end of this book)

The Four Elements of Success

Success in never a coincidence, they say. Unlike most forms of therapy that seek to understand the reasons why we feel bad or why something is not working for us, NLP focuses on what works. NLP is a model of success and its developers have studied extensively the most important factors of success. After studying countless studies and models, I have come to realize that success in practically anything in life can be crystallized on four elements.

The four elements of success are, in fact, perhaps best understood by questions that you can ask yourself:

1. **What do you want?**
- What is the worthy goal that you want to achieve?

> *"If you do not know where you are going, any road will get you there." – Lewis Carroll*

2. **Why do you want it?**
- Do you have a genuine motivation to work on your goal? Is the goal coming from within you or is it, in fact, set by an outside authority? Does your journey toward your goal enhance your level of happiness?

> *"The most successful people are those people who truly 'believe' in what they do. Not that they just say they do. They have a passion for what they do." – Richard Bandler & John La Valle*

3. **What stops/has stopped you from reaching your goal?**
- What are your limiting beliefs? Do you have all the necessary resources to reach your goal?

"Beliefs shape the way we feel, think, and act." – Mandy Evans

4. How do you reach your goal?

-   What is your strategy and, above all, what kind of action and behavior does success require from you?

> *"Without action there's no possibility of success." -Richard Bandler & Garner Thomson*

-   Remember: there are no failures along the way, only feedback. If one way of acting is not getting you the results you want, act differently.

The main thing is: Never give up, just keep on working toward what you want.

> *"Doing the same things in the same way will only get you the same results. If you want different results, something has to change." – Hannu Pirilä*

The formula for success is, after all, quite simple, and it can be executed by anyone. Some of us have found the formula and its elements by themselves. For most of us, however, figuring out the things listed above, can be tricky (if this wasn't so, most of the people in the world would define themselves as being successful).

NLP-based Success Coaching will help you especially with these four elements. It contains, however, also a lot more when needed. You do remember that we all define by ourselves what success means to us? The purpose of Success Coaching is to not only help the client to define that, but also to provide them with assistance and insights to figure out the questions stated above.

Vision, Goals and Their Purpose

There is a difference between a vision and a dream. A dream is a wish of something that would be nice to get or attain. A dream becomes a vision, and a goal, when it has a purpose or meaning and when you set a plan and begin to act on achieving it.

Countless studies have shown that the most successful people have formed a clear vision of the dream or wish, where the person sees himself already having achieved that dream. When a person starts to live according to this vision, he has usually already started his journey toward executing his vision. What is not important at this point, is how he is going to achieve his goal, but rather the fact that he has started his journey toward it. When the goal is clear enough, the means to achieve it will appear along the way.

"When you make great, big goals — whether you get to them or not — the things that happen along the way are what makes life wonderful" - Richard Bandler

Vision

So, a good vision is, at its best, a clear and strong mental image of that situation and state when and where the important goal has been achieved. It might also be a good idea to chop the main goal into smaller sub goals that serve as motivating rewards along the way to the grand prize. How do you do that, then? Let's take an example from the world of martial arts:

Goal and Sub Goals

Let us assume that you have just started practicing some form of martial art, say taekwondo or karate, and your goal is to achieve a black belt one day. At some point, often after you have practiced your discipline for a while, but sometimes even before you start taking any lessons, you get a vision in your mind of how it will feel to achieve the black belt. You cannot, however, achieve the black belt straight after the white belt. In between the white and black belts you need to pass the graduation tests of yellow belt, green belt, blue belt and so on. These grades between the white and black belts serve as excellent sub goals. Achieving each one of them feels good and rewarding.

If your main goal is to not only achieve the black belt, but in addition to *master* your martial art, you might want to chip your sub goals to even smaller parts, like to each and every training session. Your sub goal could then be to perform every training session with the best possible intensity and to adopt your teacher's teachings as deeply as possible. In that case the reward of achieving a sub goal could be the unbelievably good feeling and mental state of knowing that you have done your utmost to achieve your main goal. This applies especially to those who have what is called in NLP a strong internal reference, which means that these people do not so much seek for external acknowledgements, but they get their motivation internally by reaching their goals.

Purpose

Vision and goals are often essential in order to achieve success. In most cases, however, this is not enough. In addition to a great vision you most probably will also need a purpose. A purpose will give you the true motivation to work for your vision.

Ask yourself why you want to achieve your goal. And almost any reason
will do. What is most important is that it is specifically your reason.

Other people set a lot of goals to many of us. At work it is probably
our boss, for schoolchildren a lot of goals and expectations are being
poured over by teachers and parents. Only very few of us, however, are
really motivated by the goals set by other people. And even if it
sometimes seems like that is the case, when we look at it more closely,
we almost without exception notice that behind the real motivation is
a goal we have set for ourselves.

Sometimes when you look at things on the surface level you might think
that the goals that are set by your employer motivate you to work hard.
But when you start to dig in a bit deeper you might come to realize that
the true reason for your motivation lies inside you.

Maybe your goal is to get acceptance from your boss and that brings
you pleasure (external reference). In this case the feeling of pleasure is
your purpose. Or maybe you would like to advance in your career and
get a promotion, and achieving the goals set by your boss will probably
support that aim. In this case the career advancement could be your
purpose.

Whatever your purpose is, it is important that you find and recognize
it. It is also important that you do not feel guilty if your purpose is the
advancement of your career or lifting up your self-esteem. Whatever
the goal, if it enhances your happiness, it is good – as long as it's

ethically and legally acceptable. You see, the happier you are the better you can genuinely also help others.

We'll take a closer look at the purpose a bit later, in the context of The Purpose Behind Your Goals chapter.

Five Tips for Setting Goals

"If we have no worthwhile personal goals, it is easy to conclude that life itself is not worthwhile." – Bobbe Sommer

It is obvious that if you want to achieve something worthwhile in your life, you need to have worthwhile goals. That being the case, you will also need to be careful how you set your goals.

"The first thing is to decide: What do I want? When the goal is well-formed it is easier to get started to fulfill it." - Terttu Grönfors & Trygve Roos

How do you form your goals, then? What is a well-formed goal? There are five basic principles on what a well-formed outcome should be like:

1. **Stated in the positive**
- Say what you want and not what you don't want. In other words, describe the desired state that you want to be in when you get there.
- Our unconscious mind can't deal with the word "no". If you say to yourself "I don't want to be fat," your unconscious mind has to first form an idea of what it means to be fat. Trying to negate it after that is already too late.
- Therefore, you should set you your goal, for example, as: "I want to be lean. I want to see my six-pack abs," or something similar.

2. Initiated and maintained by individual

- Is your goal within your own control? If it isn't, how can you make it happen? You probably can't!

- You have to make it so that you are the controlling power in initiating and maintaining the process of getting there.

3. Sensory specific

- Visualize how it will look like, sound like and feel like when you have reached your goal. Go in your mind to that moment when you have reached your goal. Be there fully as it is really taking place. Always end the visualization with a dissociated image, meaning that you see yourself having reached that goal.

- Also, put a specific date on your goal. Give yourself enough time to reach it, but not too much. You want it to be a challenge, but still a reasonable challenge. (If on that date you still have not reached your goal, don't give up on the goal, give it a new date and continue to work your way towards it.)

4. Ecology check

- Ask yourself: "Is this good for me and for the important people in my life (family, friends, colleagues etc.)?" and "is it going to violate the rights of others?" If the answer to the first question is "yes" and to the second question "no", then you are on the right track.

- Also ask: "How will getting this goal positively affect and influence my life?" and "is there anybody in my environment who can help me?"

5. Testable

- How do you know that you have reached your goal? What

specific thing(s) will happen when you reach it? How will other people know that you have reached it?

- What difference will it make in your life to reach this goal?

Use this checklist every time when setting goals for yourself. Having the right kind of goal gets you already halfway there. It is, however, extremely important to remember that reaching goals require action. So, take your first step toward your goal immediately after you have formed it! By staying where you are you will achieve nothing.

Values and Meaning – What Is Important and Why?

In business world, values and mission statements have been discussed for a long time already – although in most cases they have been more like just words and a part of the company image, than actually guiding operators of action. If, however, we really give them some actual focus, they can have a huge significance in our lives, especially in a long run.

Very few of us have considered these things on our own personal level, though. This is a pity, since values and meanings play a remarkable role when it comes to achieving personal success and happiness.

> *"Knowing what your values are is excellent, because happiness comes from living your values every single day, regardless of how close or far away your goals may seem to be." -Paul McKenna*

Consideration of this subject is good to start by asking yourself: "what is important to me?" – and wait for the answer. As you ask yourself this question, you will probably get a small list of values like money, love, happiness, success, kids, work etc. These first values, although important, are usually more or less obvious and therefore we should not necessarily settle for them only.

We should go and examine this first list a little more deeply. You can do this by asking yourself: "what is important to me about (your value)?" or "why is (your value) important to me?" and so on. Ask these questions regarding every value on your list.

Now you start probably getting some different kind of answers, like, if money is important to you, "with money I can feed my family," "with money I can improve my quality of life," or if love is important to you, "being loved makes me happy," "having someone to love means that I care for other people" or perhaps something similar or maybe something totally different.

You can continue asking these "what is important to me about…?" and "why is (X) important to me?" questions for quite a long time per value. This way you can very often reveal some deeper values that are, in fact, more important to you than the values that first come to your mind.

After you have listed a total of about four to ten values, it is important to put them into an order of importance. This can be achieved by comparing the values in pairs.

So, take the first two values on your list and ask yourself, which one is more important? After you know the answer to that, take the one that is more important to you and make the same comparison to the third value on your list. For example, if the first two values on your list are money and love, ask yourself first: "which one is more important to me, money or love?" Let's say that you find love to be more important of those two and the third value on your list is happiness, you then ask yourself: "which one is more important to me, love or happiness?" Again, take the more important value from these two and make the comparison between that and the fourth value on your list.

Go through your whole list of values this way, all the way down to the last value. Whatever value "wins" the last comparison, is your most important value. Write it down on a new list as your Number 1 Value and strike it out from your original list.

Now go through the comparisons again with the rest of the values on your list. Whatever value "wins" this round is your second most important value. Write it down on the new list as your Number 2 Value and strike it out from your original list. Keep on working this way until you have put all your values into a hierarchy of values.

Next, it is time to examine your hierarchy of values a bit closer. Are there any value conflicts present? A value conflict may be present when one value, in one way or another, prevents the fulfillment of another value. For example, let's say that you have "freedom" as your Number 1 Value and "family" as your Number 2 Value. Now, in some level, you might feel that having a family prevents you from achieving the freedom in life that you desire and that might be a remarkable value conflict for you.

Value conflicts are not that common but they can significantly prevent us from achieving the success and happiness we desire. A value conflict can, in fact, very well be the key issue there.

Another thing to look for is if there are any values in your hierarchy that are based on avoidance of something. This is important because if there are values that are based on avoiding something, it means that your focus is then on the negative, and every time you focus on something that you don't want, you'll feel bad (we'll look at this a bit later in this book). For example, if the importance of family is based on your avoidance of being lonely, it means that at least part of your focus on family gives you, in fact, bad feelings.

What has been explained above, is a rather simple way of finding out what is important to you in life. When you examine the questions long and deep enough, you might find an answer to as big a question as what is the purpose of your life.

Whether you find your purpose of life through defining your hierarchy of values or not, it is quite beneficial for you to write your own mission statement, based on your values. A mission statement is a compressed, one or two sentences long, description of what is most important to you. It could be something like: "My mission in life is to help in a best possible way my children to start their own independent lives and live my own life to the fullest."

Okay, that might not touch you, but do write your own mission statement!

As I have stated earlier, companies have declared their mission statements for ages already. Microsoft, for example, states that their mission and values are the following: "At Microsoft, our mission and values are to help people and businesses throughout the world realize their full potential." As another example, Nike's mission statement is "To bring inspiration and innovation to every athlete in the world."

So why is finding out your values and mission or purpose in life so important? Values and purpose give you a direction. Without direction and purpose, your life – or in a company's case, their business – will easily drift to areas that do not bring you satisfaction, not to mention happiness. Values and purpose, along with well-formed goals, will help you keep the right direction in your life and in your actions. And when you keep moving toward a direction in your life that brings you the most satisfaction and pleasure, then life itself will be worth living.

To bring that business aspect along a bit more, just imagine how it would feel like to work in a company that has a clear direction and that has products or services that really matter?

"The Purpose Behind Your Goals"

"People are not lazy. They simply have impotent goals - that is, goals that do not inspire them." - Anthony Robbins

There is no question about it. Just having a goal is not enough. It's like a motor without the fuel – it just won't run. So let's take a closer look at your purpose.

You see, the fuel to keep your motor running is your purpose, your "why" you want to reach your goal. And like there are differences between different fuels (like gasoline vs. diesel oil), there are differences between purposes. The bigger your purpose, the more important it is to you, the better it will fire you up and keep you moving towards your goal.

So, what are your goals and what is your purpose? What do you want to accomplish and why? You are spending your time somehow anyway, so why not use it on something that has a meaning for you?

A good way to check if you can get your heart into your goal is to take a quiet moment and go into that future moment where you have reached your goal. Let yourself relax and visualize yourself having reached that goal. Really let yourself feel how it feels. See what you see, hear what you hear. Be in that moment, be there fully as if it is really taking place. Pay close attention to those feelings and where in your body you feel them – and what direction those feelings are moving.

As you feel those feelings and see what your life looks like when you have reached your goal, ask yourself "is this good for me and the important people in my life?" Then ask yourself "How is getting this goal positively affecting and influencing my life? Will it make me happier?

Then take those answers, and those feelings, sights and sounds with you as you return back to the present moment. Hold them in your mind and heart and write down the purpose behind your goal. Why do you want to reach that goal?

The next step is to list and prioritize your core values. This you have already done when you did the exercise in the previous chapter, haven't you?

Then read your primary goal, add your purpose – your why you want to achieve it – and check that it all fits to your value hierarchy. There should be no conflicts between your goals, purposes and values. Instead, if you find them to be in good harmony with each other, there should be nothing to stop you from achieving what you want.

Now, if every time you read your goal, and the purpose behind it, you get fired up, then you've got a worthy goal. And the more it fires you up, the more worthy of your time and effort it is.

Last, but not least: Check if your goal provides value for other people, as well. Because, as a wise man has once said:

> *"Time and time again, we find that the people who are truly satisfied and enriched in this life, the ones who have achieved what is indisputably happiness, are the ones who have sought to create value for others." - Charles S. Sanford, Jr.*

What Is Preventing Us from Achieving Our Goals?

"We are always aiming for something with our actions. Our goals can be conscious or unconscious." -Terttu Grönfors & Trygve Roos

Everything that we do really does have some kind of a goal behind it. Think about it: You go to a supermarket. The goal behind this action could be that you need food or perhaps detergent. Or maybe you go there just to "kill some time." That's a goal too.

What about just lying on a couch? Surely there's no goal behind that? There most certainly is. Your goal could be to relax or perhaps that same "killing some time." The goal could also be, as stated above, totally unconscious. The point is that behind every doing or action, there is always some sort of purpose.

If your goal is to kill some time, you might also want to ask yourself: what would be the most purposeful way of reaching that goal? Is it shopping, lying on the couch or maybe going to a gym of for a jog?

"It has been proven many times that if you do not have goals, chances are you will not be able to find what you truly want." - Shelle Rose Charvet

So, goals are important to us, as they guide our lives. Therefore, it is also important that you know what you want to achieve and, above all, why you want to achieve what you want. As already expressed in the previous chapters, that why is exactly the one thing that makes your goal worth a living.

Research has indicated that up to 90-95% of people are not consciously or systematically trying to achieve their goals. If reaching for a goal that is important to you makes your life more meaningful, then why are not more people trying to achieve their goals?

The answer is:

Limiting beliefs and paradigms.

What are they, then?

Beliefs are a person's perceptions of the reality. We all have our own belief systems that guide our thinking and actions. A limiting belief, then, is a belief or perception of the reality that limits our actions. One kind of a limiting belief could be your belief of what you can do, like "I will never learn how to drive a car" or "I will never meet the perfect partner." Most of these kinds of limiting beliefs have absolutely no correlation at all with what you are actually capable of doing or achieving.

By paradigms I mean here the thought patterns and behavioral frameworks that we consider to be correct and generally accepted. In other words: they are learned patterns and procedures that are rooted deeply in our minds. Examples of paradigms are the way you get dressed, brush your teeth, fold your arms, and – in a larger scale – even the way you make you're living. Paradigms represent, in a way, your comfort zones: they are the familiar and safe daily patterns and procedures that carry you through the day.

Since a paradigm is a kind of a deeply rooted habit or behavior, it oftentimes has the same effect as a limiting belief. This means that if by acting according to your present paradigms you are not achieving your goal or dream, you need to change your paradigms. On the other hand, behind a paradigm there is usually a belief. Therefore, by changing your beliefs you often also change your paradigms.

Sounds a bit too theoretical? Let's take again an imaginary example from the athletic world. Let us assume again that your goal is to achieve black belt in taekwondo. You practice maybe once or twice a week and the rest of your free time you spend by watching TV, eating junk food and maybe hanging around in bars. However, in order for you to pass the black belt graduation test, you would need to improve your stamina and flexibility, and also master the required techniques exquisitely. You, on the other hand, hate strength training and stretching and don't want to practice them. However, attaining a black belt requires that you have the above-mentioned skills and abilities. So, in order for you to achieve a black belt, you need to step out of your comfort zone and change those deeply rooted habits of yours - your paradigms - and train in a new way.

Where have these limiting beliefs and paradigms come from, then?

The easiest, although a bit outdated, way to explain this is perhaps by using the diagram below, created by Dr. Thurman Fleet and further adopted by Bob Proctor:

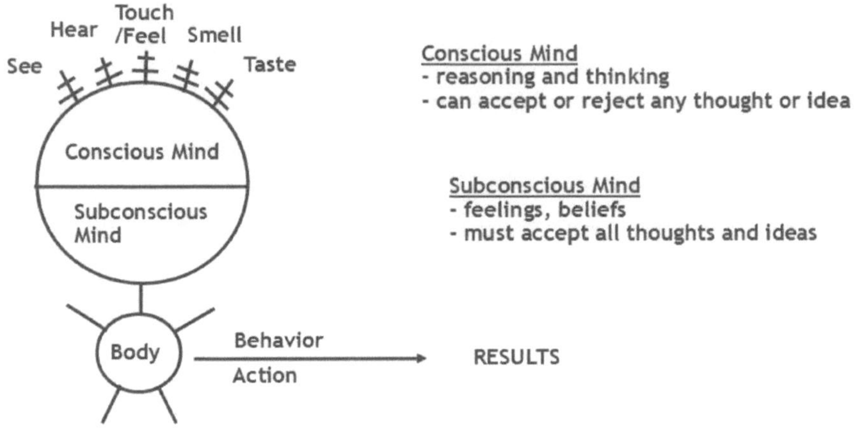

- Bob Proctor/Thurman Fleet

We observe our surrounding world through our five sensory factors, which are seeing, hearing, feeling/touching, smelling and tasting. Through these senses we have formed — and continue to form — our representation of the world. Hence, the reality that we experience is the one we have formed in our minds through our sensory factors, and all this is stored in our unconscious mind.

According to Bob Proctor and Thurman Fleet, as some kind of a filter between our senses and unconscious mind, we have our conscious mind. Our conscious mind reasons, thinks and makes conscious conclusions from all that information that we constantly receive. It can therefore, for example, reject or approve any thought or idea that we get.

Our unconscious mind, on the other hand, is not able to reject anything. It simply accepts everything that our conscious mind tells it. From all this information our unconscious mind, for example, builds us our emotional framework.

When we were little children, our conscious mind – our reasoning and thinking – was not yet developed and therefore our mind was like an open bowl. Our unconscious mind simply took in everything that was "poured into that bowl." That means that every person around us got to throw in their own ingredients to our soup of mind. In came all their beliefs and paradigms, including their beneficial beliefs and paradigms, as well as their limiting beliefs and harmful paradigms. This went on until our own reasoning and thinking faculties were developed and we slowly formed our own filters.

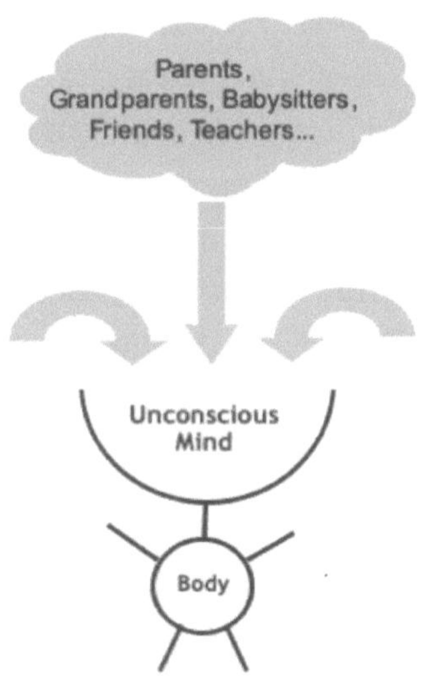

YOU AS A BABY

Unconscious Mind:
- **Has no "filters"**
- **Is like an open bowl**

In Goes:
- **values**
- **beliefs**
- **paradigms**
- **strategies...**

- Bob Proctor/Thurman Fleet

It is quite useful to understand that most of our limiting beliefs and paradigms are learned from elsewhere and that there is no way that we could have influenced on their birth and existence in our unconscious mind. And since they are so deeply rooted, changing them can be quite difficult. The good news is, however, that you can change them – no matter how old you are.

Although the view by Proctor and Fleet is in many ways based on outdated knowledge, it does illustrate the birth of beliefs and paradigms quite well.

According to what we know today, there are many other things that influence our behavior as well, like our values, so called metaprograms and anchors, to mention a few. In addition to our senses, these things form the kind of filtering system that, all combined, filter the information we receive from the outside world. In addition to all that, we have our internal processes and representations that we use to handle all the knowledge and information that we have in our brain. Therefore, the conception of Proctor and Fleet that states that our conscious mind works as a filter to our unconscious mind is unfortunately largely incomplete.

A much more accurate way to demonstrate how our communication and behavior is formed is by studying the following diagram:

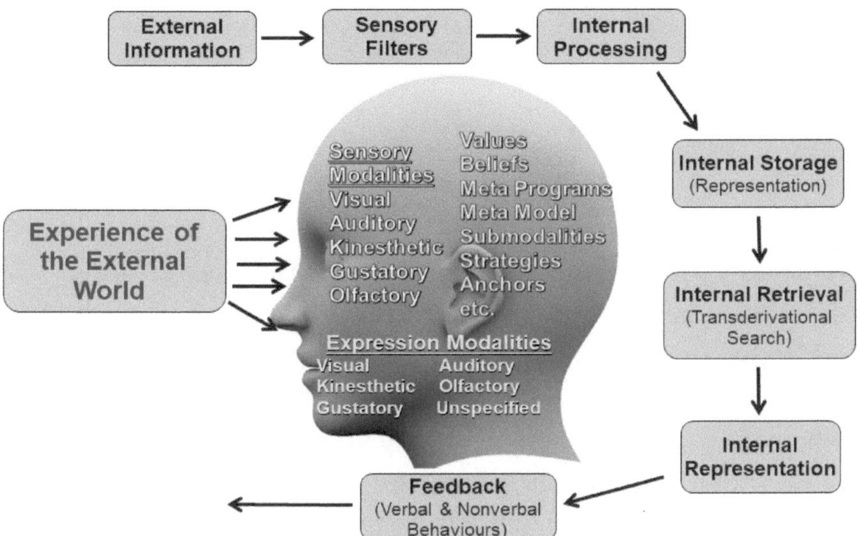

In short, we experience the world through our five senses. That information we then compare, filter and process through a number of different internal things we have formed during our lives, like our values, beliefs, strategies and, maybe in a bit more difficult terms, metaprograms, anchors and submodalities, among some other things. This is how we form our internal representation, our internal map, of the world around us. According to this internal map that we have, and which is our unique interpretation of our lives and our world, we then navigate throughout our lives.

Oh yes, and let's just say that yes, it is our unconscious mind that mainly controls our behavior — if you got a different idea from Proctor's and Fleet's views ...

Changing Beliefs and Paradigms

As far as I know, there are two main ways to change beliefs and paradigms. The traditional way is to change your conscious thinking and let the conscious mind change the perception of the unconscious mind through constant and repetitive suggestions. This, however, can sometimes take a long time to take an affect and it requires patience and determination. On the other hand, many people have provably gotten permanent results that way.

"We become what we think about." - Earl Nightingale

The other way is to use NLP techniques, which enable us to achieve changes even within minutes.

Somewhere in between these two, works hypnosis which is also used a lot as a part of NLP. In hypnosis our unconscious mind can also be fed with suggestions, but due to the altered state (or trance) we do not need as many repetitions as with the "traditional" way, described above.

"When people change what they believe in, they can change their lives." - Richard Bandler

So, if you want to change your belief that you will never learn to drive a car, you can begin to give yourself constant suggestions, like "I will learn to drive. I have all the skills and qualities that are required to drive well. I can drive well. I am a good driver." After you have repeated these suggestions several times a day for several days in a row, you will one day simply realize that you can drive a car pretty well. This is, of course, assuming that you have also practiced driving at least a little bit.

In order to use NLP techniques, you will probably need an instructor or a coach. You can learn how to perform the techniques by yourself, but I have noticed that although I knew how to instruct other people to do those techniques, doing them all by myself was far more difficult - at least in the beginning.

One important thing about changing beliefs and paradigms, though, is that in order to know what to change, you need to be aware of them. To become more aware of your way of thinking, and of your beliefs, there are two effective ways to help you with that. One is meditation and one is, again, NLP.

Meditation is an absolutely wonderful way to enhance your level of awareness and happiness. The only downside is that it takes quite a bit of time to get all the benefits from it. I have found the Holosync technology, created by Bill Harris, to be of tremendous help in getting those benefits remarkably faster.

With the help of a Licensed Trainer of NLP® or NLP Coach™ you can also become aware of the beliefs that do not serve you and also change them. That process is usually surprisingly fast and will work especially well on beliefs that are hugely limiting your life.

In order to continually improve your success and sense of happiness, I sincerely suggest that you do both: meditate daily and study NLP.

The most important message is, however, that you can change the beliefs and paradigms that are limiting your life. It might not always be easy and it will practically always require some kinds of sacrifices or efforts. But on the other hand, the rewards from making those changes can be enormous improvements in the quality of your life.

Beliefs and Their Effect on Our Lives

As I have already stated, we all have an unbelievable amount of beliefs, and most of them were formed in our childhood. Beliefs are also a very important factor in our everyday life; without them, our life would be extremely complex and difficult.

Some of our beliefs serve us well throughout our life, some limit our life unnecessarily. By changing our limiting beliefs to ones that serve us better, we change the way we think about things. How we think and what we think about, affects the emotional state we are in. Our emotional state, then, has a direct connection to how we act and behave, and the way we act and behave, produces the results we achieve in our life.

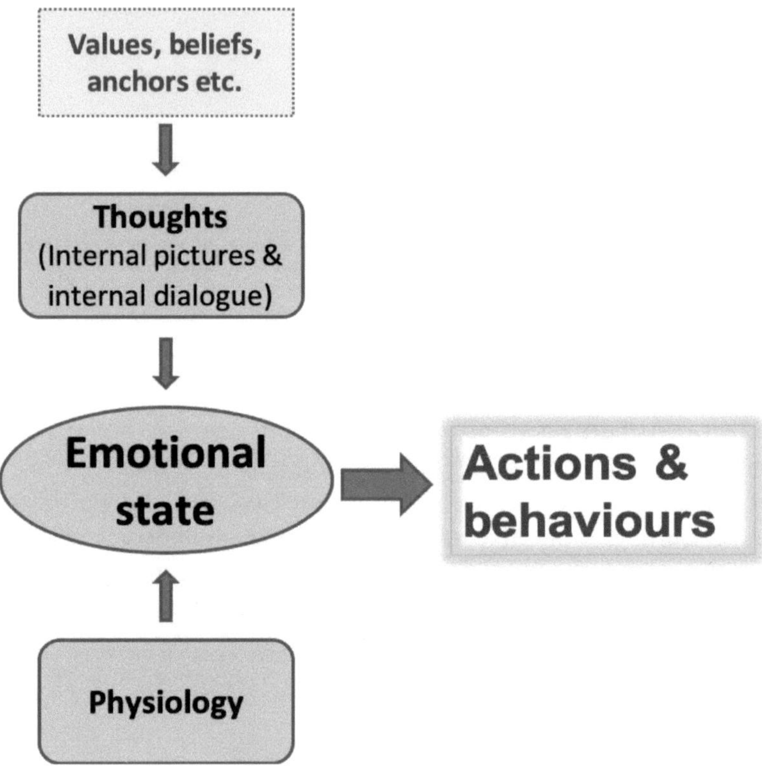

Since we have learned most of our beliefs when we were little children, many of them might turn into limitations in our life as we become adults. In fact, the single most important reason why we are not getting what we want in our life, could very well be one single un-resourceful – or in other words, limiting – belief.

In order for you to achieve different results in your life, your actions and behavior have to change. Changing your actions and behavior could, however, be extremely difficult if you don't first change your thinking and emotional states. And, as you already know now, by changing your limiting beliefs into more resourceful ones, you can remarkably change your thinking and your emotional states. So, you see already how these things are in connection with each other and what kind of powerful effect your beliefs have on your life?

Your beliefs really are only beliefs; they have nothing to do with reality. One person can believe something totally different about a certain thing than somebody else, and still, both can rationalize inside to be absolutely right, based on "facts."

So, beliefs have nothing to do with reality – beliefs are only beliefs, you understand it now, don't you?

Considering all that has been discussed above, beliefs can have a huge influence on your level of happiness and what kind of results you are getting in your life. Your beliefs can, therefore, be useful for you, or they can be ones that do not serve your purposes that well. The good news is, however, that since your beliefs are things that you have learned, you can also learn how to change them, as long as you master the right practices and techniques. And this is where NLP has the most powerful tools.

When you change your un-resourceful beliefs and thoughts into ones that serve you better, you can accomplish remarkable changes in your life.

What kind of belief or beliefs would serve you better? What beliefs do have that are not serving you or your goals? Very often, only by becoming aware of the limiting beliefs that you have, you have already started your process of changing them into more resourceful ones.

Personal Development as a Part of Professional and Career Development

We have thus far talked about personal development mostly through goals and their purposes. Let us next take a closer look at what benefits we can expect to achieve when we put some effort on our self-development.

Personal development – or self-development, or self-growth, or self-improvement, however you want to call it – can play a vital part also in your professional development.

When you develop the different areas of your human potential you can expect your career development to take a new direction upwards, as well. Getting rid of limiting beliefs or changing habits that are not serving you in a useful way will not only help you in a personal way, but they will not go unnoticed by your employer, or a potential employer, either.

People who set goals, achieve them. People who take action, get results. People who are motivated, take action. People who enjoy what they are doing are motivated. Those are all of common knowledge. Why, then, so many people are stuck in jobs they don't like and are struggling to make it through a day?

The difference is not in the genes or in the marital status or on the color of skin. It is in the attitude and how you perceive things.

When you add elements like doing work that you really like, finding a purpose for what you do and setting yourself the right kind of goals, you will not only enhance your overall happiness in life, but you will also improve your overall work performance. It is a cycle that will feed itself.

Research shows that when you do more of a particular thing, you will get better at it. When you get better at doing that thing, you start to enjoy it more. And when you enjoy it more, you want to do more of it. And, again, when you do more of it, you'll get better at it.

And the cycle goes on.

Or does it?

People do get bored on things. Especially when they are lacking a purpose for what they do and/or when there is no room for improvement anymore. Personal, and professional, development means that as you get better at what you do, you also actively seek ways to expand your awareness on what you do and how to improve and add new dimensions to it.

When you enjoy what you do, have a purpose for doing it and are actively looking for ways to accomplish more and fulfill your purpose even better, you are combining personal development with your career development.

Any smart, or even reasonable, employer will respect and value your efforts and the results that you produce. And if they don't, go find one that does.

Self-Development vs. Team-Development – Or Can They Be Combined?

Self-development has become extremely popular and it is considered to be a whole industry nowadays. Some people, however, have declared that people involved with self-development are self-centered and do not submit to the common good of all people. Is it really so?

First of all, like I pointed out in the first chapter of this book (Why Do We Need Personal Development to Be Successful?), being involved with personal development does not mean that you are self-centered. On the contrary, it means that you are developing yourself for the greater good of all humankind.

The fact of the matter is that self-development and team development can be combined and, to be precise, team development cannot be complete if it does not include self-development.

Two key components of an efficient team are the shared team purpose and team goals. Before a team member can commit to the team's purpose or goals, they must make sure that their individual purpose and goals are in line with the ones of the team. That means that a team member who has not made the effort to find out what their own purpose and goals are – meaning, has not put an effort on self-development – will not be able to commit fully on the team's objectives.

Further on, a person who is better aware of their own values, talents and potentials, who is constantly developing their own skills and abilities, and who has developed their own personal qualities like discipline, determination, consistency, patience, courage and forgiveness, is for certain more able to endow to the benefit of the team.

A person who is clear with their own needs and abilities and who sees fit with the ones of the team, is definitely a more committed team member than someone who is unsure of themself and who is "just" a member of the team. A committed team member does not count the hours. They measure the results.

Therefore, team development is not complete without sufficient amount of self-development of the individual team members. They do go hand in hand and they must be combined in order to form a team that enjoys working together, has less unproductive confrontations and goes out and produces great results. Come to think of it – isn't that the kind of a team that is called The Winning Team?

Peak Performance and Success

Peak performance is not a sole right of peak performers. Also other people than the top athletes and world famous performers need to experience their own peak performances.

We all need our own, even small, peak performances to bring enjoyment, excitement and push to our life. Without these small or big moments of peak performance, we can easily feel that there is "something missing" from our life. Without our own moments of peak performance, our life can easily become boring, benumbing and dull, won't it?

Success at almost anything requires at least some sort of peak performances. There are moments in our lives when we all would like pull out our best performance. To some, it could be in any kind of competition at any level of sport, to someone else it could be at any kind of performance in front of an audience, to yet another, it could be simply managing to get promptly, efficiently and successfully through the daily tasks.

Peak performance is not an accident, either. It requires skills and practice, but in addition to that, you also need the right kind of challenge and an optimum mental state, in which you can seize all your know-how in the best possible way.

Whatever your needs, goals or circumstances are, all peak performances require two extremely essential elements:

1. The right kind of goal, and
2. The right kind of emotional state

The Right Kind of Goal

When aiming for a peak performance, a state of flow can almost without an exception guarantee at least an excellent execution – and by the state of flow, I mean the ideal state of performance, where performing feels extremely effortless and smooth.

Mihály Csíkszentmihályi, the former head of the department of psychology at the University of Chicago, is probably the most famous researcher of flow state. Csíkszentmihályi has defined the factors that contribute to the flow state, and as the most important of them he finds to be the right balance between the requirements of the goals and the available resources (more on this subject in the next chapter).

As we have already noted several times, goals in general are a key factor in any kind of success, since they control our actions – either consciously or unconsciously. When our goal is challenging enough, yet not overwhelming, it gives us just the right kind of merit in reference to our performance and success.

The Right Kind of Emotional State

Our emotional state determines at large extent the kind of actions and behaviors we generate. Our emotional state, then, is affected mainly by two factors: our physiology and our thinking (thinking = internal representations).

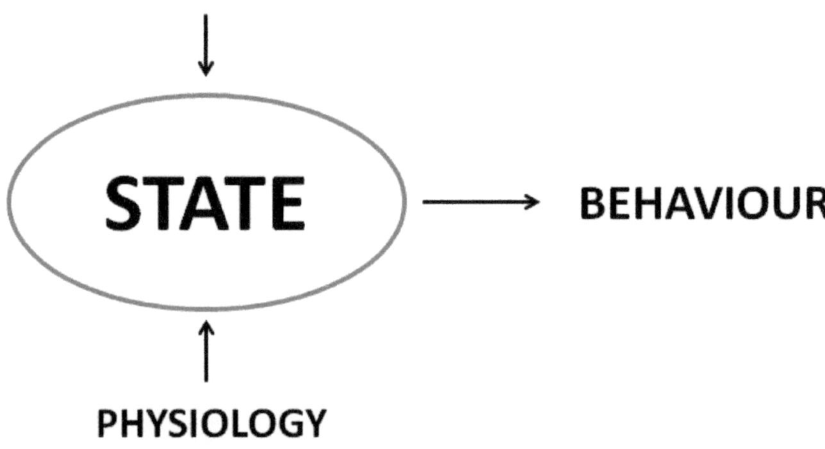

The optimal state for a peak performance requires the right kind of physiology (for example the postures of the spine and head, eyes upwards, chest out etc.), since the right kind of physiology sends the right kind of message to our brain and nervous system – say, the message of self-confidence.

Our thoughts, on the other hand, are formed mainly from our internal images and internal sounds. What kind of internal dialogue and in what tone of voice we speak to ourselves greatly affects our feelings. And so do the internal images we look at: are we looking at images of success or perhaps images of failure?

So, only by having the right kind of goals and the right kind of mental state, we can improve our performance tremendously. Naturally, there are also other factors that are present in any peak performance. However, all the factors mentioned above, as well as many other factors involved with peak performance and success, can be enhanced and practiced surprisingly fast with NLP techniques and exercises.

The above-mentioned elements and exercises are also a substantial part of the NLP based Peak Performance Coaching, which is developed to help people to achieve the success they want at practically any area of their life.

Burnout, Boreout and Flow

Some time ago the biggest newspaper in Finland had an article about the burnout of the world-famous Finnish ice hockey coach Juhani Tamminen. It is admirable that Mr. Tamminen came out in public with his burnout. What is not admirable, however, is that he had to experience it. A true burnout can be a devastating experience and I do not wish that to anyone.

Basically, a state of burnout happens when the challenges and requirements have for a long enough period of time been remarkably greater than the resources (like time, know-how etc.) available.

Another extreme state, although not much written about in media, is so-called boreout, a total boredom. A boreout happens when the resources are for a long enough period of time remarkably greater than the challenges and requirements. The consequences of boreout are very much similar to those of burnout: a person can't get anything done, they have a feeling of total emptiness.

Between burnout and boreout lies then a state which is very much desired: the state of flow, when everything seems to be running like a dream. This state can be achieved when the challenges and requirements are in optimal balance for performance. This is also an extremely enjoyable state to work in, whether you are performing in sports, in front of an audience, in a work situation or practically in any other event in life.

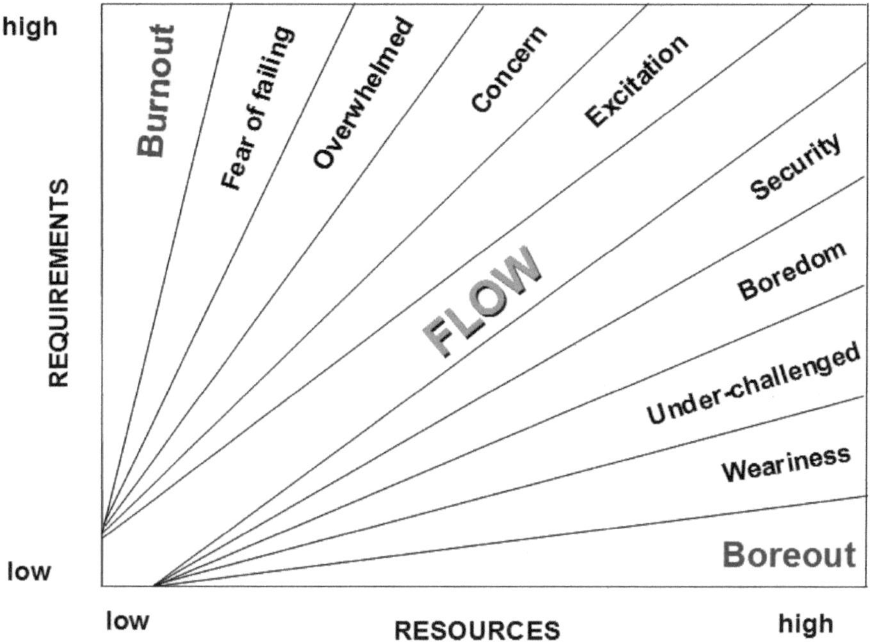

Reaching the state of flow is not an automated act. However, the chances of reaching it can be remarkably enhanced. The most important thing is that the challenges and requirements are in optimal balance with the resources available. Since keeping this balance in the optimal level at all times is practically impossible, we tend to, even in ideal circumstances, constantly move somewhere between the states of excitation and security.

In order to reach the state of flow more frequently it is important to recognize when the requirements start to cause stronger negative feelings like concern. When that happens, either the level of requirements should be lowered or – perhaps even better – the resources available be increased, in the form of additional training or time, for example. Correspondingly, if signs of feelings like boredom start to appear, a person should get more challenges as soon as possible.

Recognizing these signs can sometimes be difficult, especially if all the people around you are also busy with their own tasks and doings. Therefore, using a professional mentor or coach might very well be the best thing to do in order to keep you operating in the peak level of performance and enjoyment and in order to avoid burnout or boreout.

Feeling Bad vs. Feeling Good

So far we have discussed mainly success, happiness, peak performance and other toward-goals related subjects. Let's now take a short look at the darker side of life: bad feelings

Bad feelings – whether they come in the form of worries, fears or even panic attacks – are based on one, and only one, thing: Our attention at those moments is focused on things we want to avoid. Every time we think of something we do not want in our life, we feel bad. Sometimes the feeling can be mild, but sometimes the feeling can be even overpowering.

The process of feeling bad and feeling good is basically the same. As you already know, our thinking is mainly based on internal images and internal sounds. If you, in your mind, look at pictures of unpleasant things – things you don't want in your life – or you talk to yourself in a negative tone of voice about negative things, these thoughts cause you to feel bad, even physically.

If, however, you look at images about things you like and enjoy and want to have more in your life or talk to yourself in a pleasant tone of voice about pleasant things, the effect is the opposite.

When you add to this your body posture – closed and hunched posture vs. vigorous and open posture – you pretty much have the whole package put together.

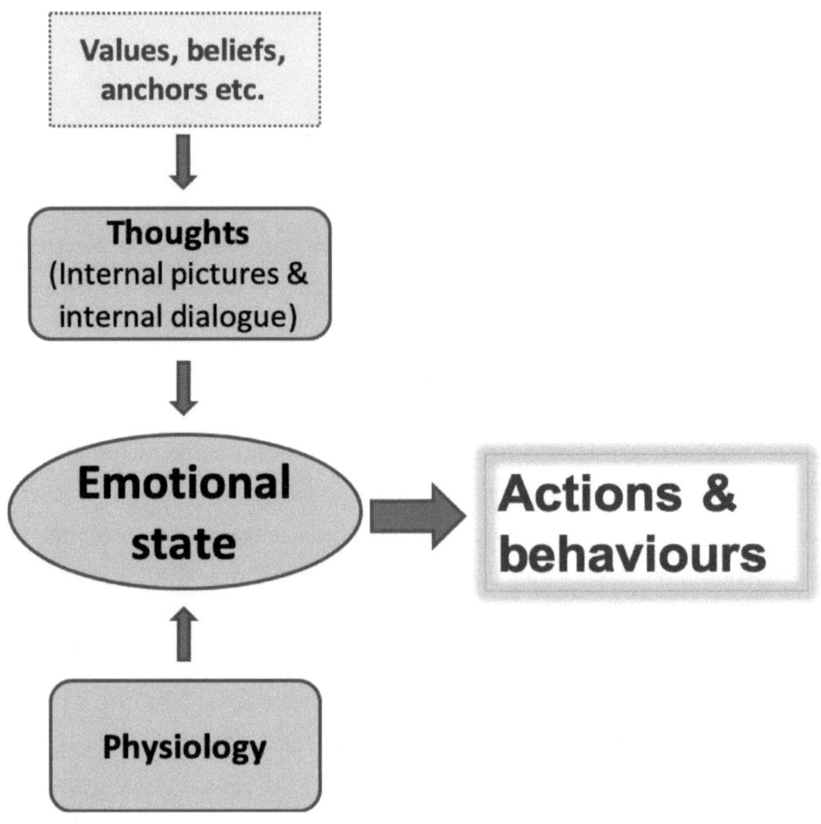

An interesting question then arises: who is in charge of your thoughts and body postures?

The answer is, of course: you are.

But is it really that simple?

During our life, we have learned a huge amount of different kinds of habits, conditionings, anchors, beliefs, strategies and who knows what, that have all, at the moment they were created in our mind, served or protected us. Some of the habits and beliefs, that once were useful for us, might not necessarily be that way anymore in other situations in our life. Still, we might have formed, in our unconscious mind, a resemblance or equivalence between things, even based on one single experience. These habits and beliefs might then have become limitations to us, limiting our freedom of choice on what and how to think. And all this is usually happening automatically, guided by our unconscious mind.

When you want to get rid of the worries, fears or even panic attacks, you need to teach your brain to think in a new way. There are numerous techniques to do this, but in the end, it is really all about that one thing: Instead of thinking about what you don't want to happen, you need think about what you *want* to happen."

I had a client who got a panic attack every time he thought about crossing a bridge by car. In fact, he had had it for about five years. He created his panic by creating in his mind pictures of how he loses control of his car and crashes down off the bridge. First, I taught him to neutralize the sense of panic by changing these images he saw in his mind from what he did not want to happen to images about what he wanted to happen (ie. him driving safely across bridges). Even by doing only this, he reported a week later that he had been able to drive across several bridges without a hint of a panic attack! In the next phase we then concentrated to direct his thoughts even more toward the things he wants in his life. As a result, he learned to have a lot less bad feelings and instead, a lot more good feelings in his life.

Even though the difference between whether we feel good or bad is very simple, making the necessary changes by ourselves might be a bit challenging. Luckily, NLP offers amazingly effective methods and techniques for making the appropriate changes. In my profession, mastering these techniques has produced me the most rewarding experiences one after the other, bringing me an ever growing enthusiasm to keep on doing what I'm doing. And those thoughts bring me very good feelings.

More Good Feelings, Less Bad Feelings

I have often been asked, how can one really change a bad feeling to a good feeling?

Unfortunately, I don't really have any single, one-fix-for-all, answer or technique to that. Even NLP has hundreds of techniques that are all intended, in one way or another, to bring us better and more useful mental states, which cause us to act and behave in more useful ways, thus bringing us better results in our life.

However, as a first step, we could consider of becoming more aware of our states. If we want to get rid of bad mental states and get good mental states instead, we need to be aware of these states. When you realize that you are in a bad mental state – experiencing bad feelings – you can take some actions to change it. Many of us don't even recognize their bad mental states but live in them from day to day as like being driven by an autopilot. To become more aware of your mental states might be helped by the use of meditation or Mindfulness, which both will help you to be more in the present moment and become more aware of yourself. Many forms of trances and relaxation exercises can also be very helpful in this.

If you feel that this "becoming aware" stuff is a too difficult or heavy process, then help from a professional coach might be the best choice for you to get you started with it. A professional NLP Coach might be able to help you very fast to become aware of any factors that might limit your thoughts, feelings or actions, and help you to change them into more useful and better serving ones for you.

Being aware of these mental states is very important, however. If you don't know what you want to change, changing it will be quite difficult.

I recently helped a client who had a long list of things (approximately 20 things) she wanted to have changes to. The list included things like all kinds of social fears – and fears in general – all kinds of anxiety and depression, heavy tiredness and strengthlessness, problems in mind control, insomnia and many others. In these cases, it is usually important to first clarify what is important in life in general. So, we started by finding out about my client's value hierarchy. It came as no surprise to me that she had tremendous difficulties to tell what the most important things in her life were. She had never really thought about it.

After we had clarified her values and hierarchy of values, we noticed that there were some conflicts in them. Also, her three highest values were based on avoidance of things and the fourth value was the first that was based on good feelings. As I mentioned earlier, if our focus is on things we want to avoid, we have a lot of bad feelings as a result.

In my client's case, as it oftentimes is, these top three values that were based on avoidance and the fourth value in her hierarchy, all had the same underlying good purpose behind them. Behind them all was a purpose that was to bring her safety and comfort – the purpose was just directed in a negative way. After she realized this, we performed an NLP technique called "Visual Squash", which triggered very strong emotions and insights in my client.

This was a good start and the process of change had started. In addition to Visual Squash, we performed several other NLP techniques as well, including the "Logical Levels". As a result, there was an evident change in my client: she was clearly relaxed and relieved, her face had now a healthy color and she, in fact, looked 10-15 years younger. All this in less than two hours. My client was also somewhat confused because she was not able to access the things that used to unnecessarily worried her so much. Instead of all the problems, she now had started to see *solutions* to her problems, in addition to a direction toward better feelings.

All in all, these are not very complicated things. The question is pretty much about learning a new strategy, a new way of thinking and seeing things. Where we used to be so attached to the strategy of thinking – which we had learned way back in the past – that caused us to create bad feelings, we can now learn a new strategy, a new thinking process, that brings us solutions and good feelings. When we become aware of these strategies that are not serving us well, the change process to something better can begin.

So, what is my advice?

- Stop and relax, meditate. If you keep up a constant hurry and stress, it is very difficult to become aware of your own thoughts – if not even impossible.
- Know what you want, what is important to you. If your thoughts circle around the things that you want to avoid in your life, think what are the things that you want instead, to which direction do you want to go?

And, like I said, if you feel that the process is too long or cumbersome, do contact a competent NLP Coach or sign up to an NLP course. You might be amazed at how remarkable changes can be achieved in a very short period of time.

My Truth vs. Your Truth

Probably each of us has sometimes encountered situations in our lives where we wonder, how in the world does that other person not understand me at all or what I mean? Or "how can that person say such things?" or "why on earth does that person behave that way?"

The reason for all this is that we each look at this world as if through "our own truth". We all have our own truth about every situation and every matter and for someone else that "truth" is quite different than for me, for example.

So your "truth" is different from my "truth."

For someone, for example, a deserted beach can be quite an awful place because there are no other people there. Someone may find the place lonely and boring, for instance. Someone else, on the other hand, finds the same place absolutely wonderful because they are allowed to be at peace.

Our own "truth" is greatly influenced by e.g. what we consider important, what our values are. For example, do you value social contacts or do you value the fact that you can be alone in your own peace?

Thus, values really play a big role in the formation of our own truth.

Another significant factor is our beliefs – what we believe about ourselves, other people and this world around us. Is the world good or bad, are people good or bad? Who am I, what do I do? What kind of person I am?

So, for example, when you sometimes encounter a person who you think is treating you unfairly and you are horrified at how they can treat you that way, their truth can simply be completely different from your truth. Their values and beliefs don't seem to fit in with your values and beliefs. Maybe they believe about themself something that influences their behavior in that situation.

We all have, in a way, our own map, our own model of the world, by which we navigate through our lives and by which we act in our environment the way we act. This map of ours is also always completely unique, we each have a map of our own, and it is good to understand and realize that a person who behaves badly towards you does not necessarily mean anything bad about it. They simply don't think the same way you do – their thinking doesn't work the same way you think because their map, their model of the world, is quite different.

When we learn to understand that we each have our own unique model of the world and that we each think and act in our own way and value different things and that we believe differently about different things (plus a whole bunch of other factors), we may have it a little easier to accept the behavior of others.

On the other hand, it is also good to recognize that we ourselves may not always be right. That "truth" of ours is not really the truth. It is just our perception of the truth.

In fact, none of us really knows what that real truth is, for we always look at the world through our own "lenses". And these lenses of ours are made up of many different factors: they are affected by e.g. our values, our beliefs, our so-called meta-programs and a lot of other things.

So the next time you meet a person and you think, how in the hell does that person behave that way, why don't they understand me, why do they do things like this to me? – maybe it would be better to think that "hmm… what is in that person's model of the world that makes him behave like that?"

When we understand even a little bit of the other person's model of the world, we may also find there things that help us get our own message across in a way that other person accepts our view better.

These are all things that affect our communication and that we go over in NLP a lot and what we explore in NLP. In fact, with NLP, these things get often solved and we are able to communicate better with each other.

So what is your truth? What is the truth of your friends or relatives? After all, we all have our own truths…

The Point behind Self-Help Books

One of the easiest and most inexpensive ways to study is reading books. The number of self-help, or self-improvement, books on the market is increasing all the time. Why is that? Who reads them anyway?

In some ways, self-help books have existed for a long time, from the first "code of conduct" books to modern self-improvement or personal development books. But when you start to think of it, probably the most read self-help book was written centuries, even a couple of thousand years ago. And that is the Bible.

There are nowadays so many different kinds of self-improvement books on the market that it has become quite difficult, especially for a beginner, to choose which ones to read. While it is impossible to give an all-embracing advice for that, there are, however, a couple of things you might want to consider when deciding what to read:

> **1. Look/ask for recommendations** from people you trust and admire. Ask you coach or mentor, discuss about the books in web forums, read self-improvement/personal development websites. Many people are more than happy to give you recommendations.

> **2. Go with your gut feeling.** Go to a bookstore or library and browse around the self-help section. Read the book covers and just pick a book that for some reason

appeals to you. Oftentimes, your unconscious mind knows the best.

The main point, however, is to read them. I suggest that you read different kinds of self-help books, at least until you'll get the feel of what suits you best. Then read some more of that. And then, after a while, go and explore again.

I think it is important that you find out what works the best for you and then really dig deep into that. But don't get too caught up in just one particular way or style of self-improvement. Broaden your perspective every once in a while.

It is also important to realize that even though reading a lot of self-help books will motivate you and give you great insights, the books cannot give you everything. The books are always targeted to masses, not to an individual person. In order for you to get ahead most effectively in your personal development, I strongly suggest that you get yourself a mentor or a coach. Even just a few meetings with a good coach will help you tremendously and give you a good boost to the right direction (more on this subject later on in this book).

The self-help books will support you in your endeavors and give you good additional advice but, in my opinion, they cannot give you the personalized pieces of advice that you can get from a coach or a mentor. And don't forget to ask your coach for good book recommendations!

How to Live a Happier Life

There are a lot of great pieces of advice on how to have a better life, how to be happier and so on. Some say: "Think positive," others encourage you to "look at the bright side of everything." While all this is helpful and true, in a way, what it all comes down to at the end is: "Do things that you love doing."

"Easier said than done," you say? "I have to work, take care of the kids, take them to their hobbies, feed them, clean the house etc." How can you find the time to do what you love to do?

Well, there are basically two ways of making the change. Either you take some "baby steps" or you make a huge change at once. Whatever works best for you. Some people need to make a radical change, but for some making small changes is a better choice. However you do it is up to you, but the fact remains that you need to do things that you love doing, in order to live a happier life.

Think of a target board, where you have a center and three rings around the center. The outermost ring of the target represents things that are not urgent and not important to you. These could be things like watching TV, hanging out with friends, reading comic books or something similar.

The next ring towards the center represents things that are urgent but not important. These are the petty things that sometimes seem run some people's lives. They are often things that are requested by other people but have no real importance to you. They often make you feel important and busy, but in the end, they don't really serve you or your goals.

The third ring towards the center represents things that are important and urgent. These are mainly the important things that you have to *react* upon, things like taking care of an injured child or a sudden opportunity to do a project or a task that you really enjoy taking.

Then there is the center of the target. These are the things that are important but not urgent. This is the *proactive* area of your life, where you are working on things that you really enjoy and love doing, but don't have the urgency attached to them. This is where you plan and create things.

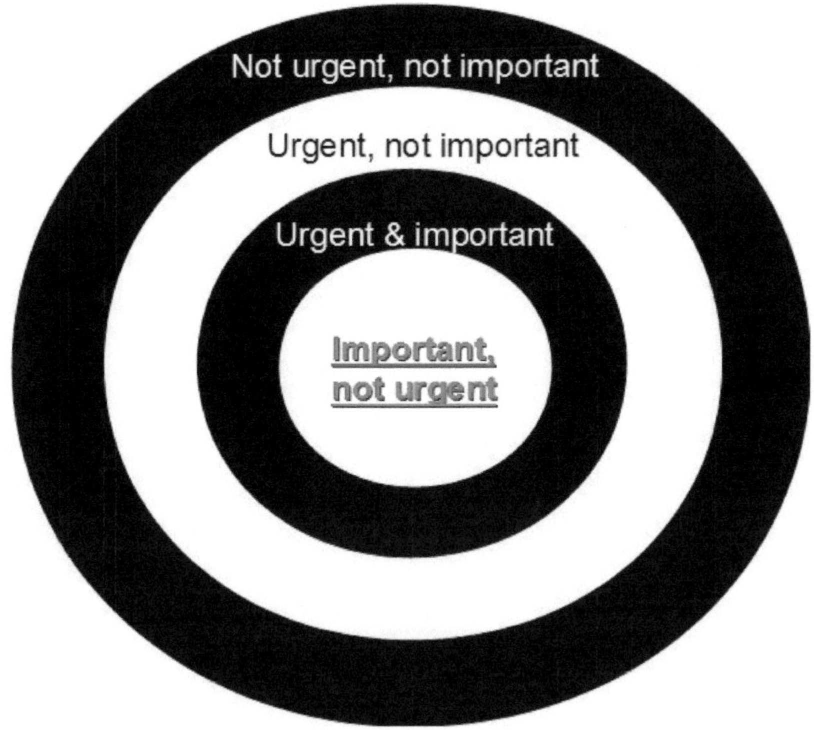

In order for you start building the life you want, the happier life, you need to spend more time on the things in the center of the target. You need to spend more time doing things that are important to you, but not urgent. That is not to say that you need to stop spending time on the other areas, but more like starting to increase the amount of time you spend on the things in the center.

How can you do that when life is so hectic and you just can't find the time to do that? The answer is: you need to prioritize. There are a lot of time management programs available, so I am not going to get in too much detail on that subject. There are, however, some extremely useful questions you can ask yourself whenever you are writing your to-do lists or having a battle on what to do next. Ask yourself:

- "Is this really important to *me*?"
- "Is doing this taking me toward *my* goals?"
- "Is this promoting a *happier* life for *me*?"

Answering these questions might not bring an instant improvement to your life, but if you start asking yourself these questions constantly, you will soon notice a change in what you do and how you look at things.

And don't worry about becoming too selfish if you start paying more attention to your own needs and desires. If you want to make other people's lives happier, you first have to be happy yourself. You cannot give others what you don't have.

Letting Go as a Vital Part in the Universal Cycles of Change

I am well aware that the title of this chapter may sound a bit vivid but bear with me – this subject is extremely interesting and important.

The Universal Cycles of Change – the natural process that describes how everything in the whole universe evolves – has seven stages:

1. **Creation** – the starting point of every process of change.

2. **Growth** – the realization, or the shape forming, of the creation.

3. **Complexity to Maturity** – the reach of a "steady state" when the system operates at its best.

4. **Turbulence** – the becoming of too complex in growth and development to operate at optimal level.

5. **Chaos** – the beginning of falling apart.

6. **Droppings Off** – the letting go of the un-serving parts.

7. **Meditation & Inward Silence** – the state of renewal and rejuvenation.

The Universal Cycles of Change

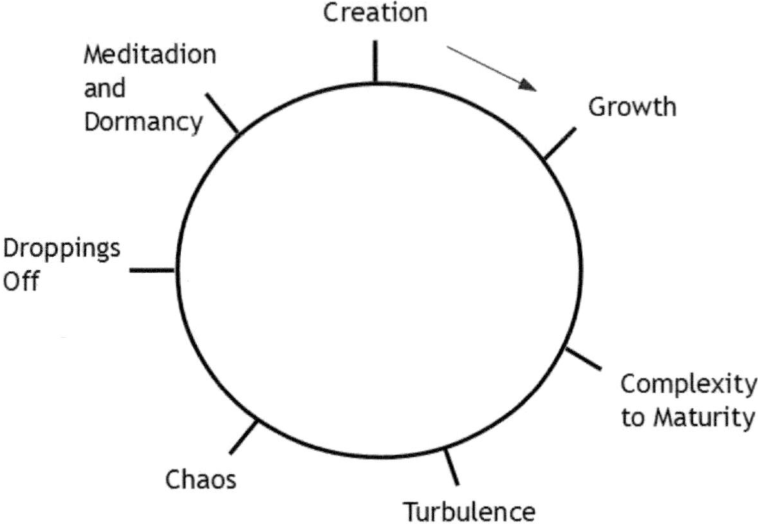

Everything in the universe – and in life – has to go through this cycle in order to keep evolving, renewing or developing to a higher state. You might notice the stages in your own growth cycle with some of the following signs:

If you want to get yourself a better life, in one way or another, the first step is to **create** a vision of the life you want and goals that you want to achieve along the way to that vision.

Then you have to take action to reach your goals. You start the construction process of your vision and your vision starts to take shape. You **grow** toward that vision of yours, like a tree starts to sprout from a seed.

As you reach your goals, several things run smoothly and you are on the roll. You reach a state of "flow." Your idea has reached **maturity**.

As you reach more and more of your sub-goals you start noticing that things get more and more difficult to handle. You start to grow out of your present limits, which causes **turbulence**.

You reach the point where you can't keep all the balls in the air anymore. You have added too many balls to your juggling act. Things are getting **chaotic**.

You have to **let go** of the things that don't serve you and your vision in the most beneficial way anymore. Like a snake has to shed its skin or a three has to drop its leaves, you need to get rid of the old habits and beliefs that are preventing you to grow further.

After the dropping off you need to **recuperate**. Go inside and get ready for a new creative process to take place. Take a deep breath and gather your strengths again. The cycle is about to commence again.

Many of us start the process without much difficulties. We sail through the cycle to the point of turbulence or chaos. And hit a brick wall. So many of us don't know how to let go of the old beliefs that used to serve us so well but are now blocking our growth and journey toward our vision. For too many of us, dropping off is the hardest part.

If you look at anything in the nature, you notice that us humans are the only creatures in the universe that have difficulties with dropping off of what is preventing our growth. We tend to hang on to the useless stuff we have gathered. And we most definitely hang on to the beliefs we have learned as kids. Those beliefs served and protected us

so well when we were kids, but as we grow older, many of those beliefs
are not serving us anymore. They become our limitations, our limiting
beliefs.

*"In order to change, we must be willing to give up the old way of
being. If the way we see things does not change, if we hang on to
the old, we will continue to get the same results." - Bill Harris*

There are many ways and techniques on how to change those limiting
beliefs. Maxwell Maltz describes a six-week process in his book about
Psycho-Cybernetics. There are, however, a lot faster ways to reach the
same outcomes. NLP has proven that it is possible to change those
limiting beliefs even within minutes.

There are several self-study books about the belief change processes
and techniques, like the Maltz's Psycho-Cybernetics, but if you'd like
to get results fast and effectively, I highly recommend that you consult
an experienced NLP practitioner or NLP coach. I further suggest that,
since there are all kinds of "so-called" NLP practitioners around, you
also make sure that the NLP practitioner has been licensed by the co-
creator of NLP, Dr. Richard Bandler, himself.

*The Universal Cycle of Change concept is created by Kris Hallbom, the co-founder
of the NLP Institute of California.*

How to Generate a Change in Life?

By doing the same things in the same way, you can only achieve same results. If you want something in your life to change, you have to do something in a new way. If you want to do something in a new way, it also requires a change in your thinking.

For many people, change, even a small one, is horrible. The sameness in the environment and activities creates a sense of security. But what if doing things differently would make things better, even safer? Most of the time, you won't know it unless you really give it a try.

If you now stop for a moment now to think of something that you would like to be better in your life, then what would that thing be? Maybe you can find more than one thing.

How long have you wanted that change? What have you done to bring about that change? What would happen if you actually implemented the change? These are questions that often preoccupy many.

Before you carry out any change, especially anything more significant, you should first consider whether that change is necessary at all or even good for you. The best way to figure it out is to go in your mind and look at the future and see and experience the consequences of the change.

Therefore, do the following (read the instructions completely before doing this exercise):
- Define the change you would like to make.

- Specify the moment when you would like that change to take place (note that this does not bind you to anything – you do not have to make your change by a certain date).

- Take a few deep breaths, close your eyes lightly and relax.

- Think of the moment in the future when that change has taken place and step into that moment. Quite physically, if you like, take a step or two and step into that moment in the future.

- As you step into that moment, see where you are. What is the environment, what does it look like there? What has changed in that environment now that you have made that change? What things are better now, is something worse? Who else is there? What do they look like, what do they do? Conceive everything you can see around you as well and genuinely as possible.

- Still staying in that environment and moment, next pay attention to what sounds you hear. Are there birds singing, roar of the waves, or something else? Are there people's voices? If so, what do they say and what is their tone of voice? Are you perhaps saying something to yourself, either out loud or in your mind? If so, what and in what tone?

- While still staying in that moment and environment, pay attention to any odors or tastes. Can you smell the sea or a taste of champagne or something else?

- Finally, pay attention to your feelings. How do you feel now that you've made that change? Where in the body is that feeling and what is that feeling (is it tingling, warmth, coldness, pressure, palpitation, or something entirely else)? How does that feeling move in your body?

- Now that you are experiencing that situation with all your senses, consider for a moment what things that change will bring along:
  - What good will it do for you?

- o What are the side effects for you?
    - o What good does it bring to your environment and other people?
    - o What are the side effects it has on your environment and/or other people?
  - After reflecting these things for a moment and you're finished, you can take the steps back to where you originally were and open your eyes.

After experiencing as vividly as possible everything the change will bring along, take a pen and paper and write down the answers to a few questions:

- What **happens** if you **carry out** the change?
- What **happens** if you **do not** carry out the change?
- What **does not happen** if you **carry out** the change?
- What **does not happen** if you **do not** carry out the change?

As you now look at the answers you've written down, it should be very clear to you whether you should implement that change or not. If you don't find it worthwhile, then simply forget the whole thing or make alterations to your planned change and do the exercise again. If, on the other hand, you find it worthwhile to implement that change, then implement it.

How to carry out the change, then?

The implementation of change depends, of course, on where you are at the moment and where you are going with your change. The most important thing is that you know that the change is good for both you and your environment, and that you've already figured out. The next step is to make a plan for the change. There are, of course, many different ways to do this. Here's one that is quite easy and functional:

- Go back in your mind to that moment when you have made the change. See what you see then; hear what you hear then; feel what it feels like then. Really experience that situation as vividly as you can.
- Next, think of some sort of timeline so that the past is behind you and the future is in front of you and you are now in the future moment when you have just made the change you want.
- Turn around and look back at the timeline of the past from that future moment and notice what things must have happened between that future moment and the present to make that change come true. What actions have you taken? Who have you been in contact with, where did you get help or information from, what concrete steps have you taken? Mark all the things that come to your mind on the timeline in a way that is most appropriate for you.
- Once you have marked enough things on your timeline, turn around again so that the past (including the present) is behind you again. Recall what it looks, sounds and feels like when you've made the change.
- Start going backwards from that future moment to the present, noting the things that have happened along the way that you have marked on your timeline.
- When you reach the present, stop. Standing at the present, look at the timeline in front of you and the things you will do to you fulfill the change you want. If needed, make further adjustments to that plan.
- When you are happy with your plan, make a **decision** to implement the plan and the change.
- Note what your first step will be and decide when you will take

it.

- Step aside from the present on your timeline. Your plan is ready. It's time to start implementing the change you want.

If you need more NLP tools for making a change, you can get very effective ones at the Licensed Practitioner of NLP™ training. NLP is a technology of change that allows you to remove your mind's limitations that have prevented you from making the change you want to implement. The bigger the change, the more you will benefit from NLP.

Five Reasons Why (at Least) an Entrepreneur Should Have a Mentor or a Coach

In this book I have mentioned several times a Mentor or a Coach. Although this chapter is directed mainly to entrepreneurs, these same things apply to all of us who want to enjoy our lives more, succeed better at our work or do work that has meaning to us and others.

Being an entrepreneur is often a 24/7 job. Depending on your passion on what you do, it can truly feel like an overwhelming amount of work or it can be your life's fulfillment. A good mentor or a coach can help you with either.

An entrepreneur is very often lacking the massive resources that an executive of a large corporate has available practically immediately. On the other hand, an entrepreneur can usually make quick changes to their operations to respond to the needs of the market.

Since an entrepreneur very often lacks the support and benefits of a management team, they are often going through the days with more limited and narrower view on things around. What an entrepreneur needs is a mentor or a coach to guide them in the achievements of their dreams. Here are five reasons why any entrepreneur – and many others – should have a mentor or a coach:

> **1. A good mentor/coach asks questions that broaden your view.** You should not view things only on your perspective. In order to make changes you need to view things on different perspectives to avoid narrow-

mindedness. Having different perspectives on things will give you clear advantages against your competitors.

2. A mentor/coach can point out where to find information. A mentor is not a person who has all the answers, but a good mentor should be able to give you advice on where to get the answers and help that you need. You should not spend hours and days pondering on questions you don't have the expertise on. Find someone who knows better.

3. A mentor/coach can help you enjoy your work more. Are you passionate about your work? Are you excited every day to get to work? A good mentor can help you find your passion. When you are excited about your work you achieve more and your brain has more positive chemicals to produce better results.

4. A mentor/coach is a good sounding board. Very often, just to speak out your plans and ideas to someone who listens and understands what you are talking about will help you come up with better solutions by yourself. By throwing a few targeted questions a mentor can help you realize the answers that you already have within you.

5. A good mentor/coach has a big "toolbox." Mentoring and coaching is not only about listening and asking the right questions. Quite often a mentor needs to have real tools and exercises that will help you make the progress you need. Sometimes you need actual tools and answers to your problems and a good mentor will provide them to you. In one way or another.

If you are an entrepreneur and you don't have a mentor or a coach yet, go get one. Finding the right one for you might take a while sometimes but being without one can cost you a lot more. Go ask around, get references, have a few meetings with one. You'll know when you've found a good one. Just go get one.

Six Self-Improvement Tips You Cannot Afford to Ignore

The world around us is constantly evolving. Okay, maybe you don't consider all the evolution being an improvement, but the fact is that since change is inevitable, we need constant self-improvement, as well, if we want to keep up with the rest of the world.

Sometimes the demands of the modern world can also seem like an overwhelming task to live up to. For many people it really is like that. There are, however, a few tips that can guide you to a self-improvement path that will not overload your mind and will only take little of your everyday time. If you follow these six self-improvement tips, I guarantee you that you can conquer the demands set by the outside world:

1. Decide what you really want. Are you running in a rat race trying to live up to other people's expectations or are you engaging in activities that bring you pleasure and satisfaction? As the saying goes: "You only *have to*, until you *want to*. Then you don't *have to*, anymore." Do what you love doing and it doesn't seem like work at all.

2. Make sure your goals are set in the positive. Imagine you tell a taxi driver that you want to get away from here – wherever that may be. Where would he take you? Anywhere. If you give your mind the same kind of instruction it would most probably take you to a similar kind of place as where you left from. Why? Because it would be a familiar place. That's how your mind works. It is drawn to what is familiar – even when it's not good for you. By only avoiding things you don't want, you still have not defined where you want to go. List the things you **want** in your life, not the ones you don't want.

3. Know your purpose. "When you've got a big enough why, you'll find any how." Having a positive goal is not enough. You also need to know why you want to achieve that goal. That gives you the motivation for your self-improvement. Like Tony Robbins says: "People are not lazy. They simply have impotent goals - that is, goals that do not inspire them."

4. Study NLP. NLP has the modern knowledge of how your mind works and the latest and most effective techniques to make those changes that you need to make. Remember: You cannot get new results with old habits and beliefs – something has to change in order for you to get new results. And NLP has the tools for that.

5. Spend more time on what is important but not urgent. Pay attention to how you spend your time. Most of us spend too much time on things that are both important and urgent ("putting out fires," being in stress) or on things that are neither important nor urgent (just being "lazy"). While both are important – because there are things that you just need to do and you do need to take some time to relax, too – spending time on things that are important but not urgent, is where your self-improvement happens. Read inspiring books, study, meditate… Things like that.

6. Get yourself a mentor/mentors or a coach/coaches. Although self-improvement is about you, you do need someone to guide you. It is extremely difficult – if not impossible – for you to keep an open mind and see the best path to take just by yourself. During your lifetime you have formed an enormous amount of habits and beliefs that are not serving you in the most useful way. Without a good mentor or coach it is practically impossible for you to recognize all those limiting habits and beliefs. And even more difficult to change them to more useful ones.

Follow these tips and you are guaranteed to see remarkable improvements in your life. Without exceptions.

Briefly About NLP

I have mentioned NLP several times in this book. NLP is an abbreviation of Neuro-Linguistic Programming. The word "neuro" refers to the neurologic processes in us, ie. the processing of information that happens in our brain and mind. "Linguistic," then, refers to our verbal and non-verbal communication, through which we communicate, both consciously and unconsciously. "Programming" refers to the structure of our thinking and how we have programmed ourselves to think and behave, and, especially, how we can achieve better results by altering certain structures in that programming.

NLP was originally developed by Richard Bandler and John Grinder in early 1970's. Bandler got the impulse to create NLP when he realized how psychology and different forms of therapy were so inadequate in delivering practically any help to people in need for it. Together with Grinder, Bandler studied and modeled those few therapists who, for some reason, were able to get positive results in a more regular basis with their patients. Some of the therapists they modeled were, among others, Milton Ericksson, Virginia Satir and Fritz Perls.

After modeling capable therapists Bandler and Grinder went on to model also other top experts in their fields: Olympic athletes, corporate executives, top salespeople, artists and so on. Bandler and Grinder noticed that the unconscious skills and strategies of these top performers' minds can be modeled and also taught onwards to other people. Thus, they formed an understanding on how the human brain works and how other humans can be taught to think and behave in a way that is more useful and appropriate for them.

In NLP, the objects of interest are not the problems and their history, but rather the skills, competencies, successes and their structures. Most of all, NLP is a technology that can help people create the changes they desire.

Unfortunately, there are all kinds of trainings out there that are called by the name of NLP. Regrettably, I have met all kinds of practitioners, and even "trainers," of NLP who are trained only on a very small part of NLP – and even those who speak of NLP as something it is not.

Richard Bandler is undeniably the father and developer of NLP. For about 50 years now Dr. Bandler has also developed NLP further, due which the NLP that Bandler represents nowadays is much more than what it was in the beginning when he started it with John Grinder. Therefore, the practitioners and trainers of NLP who are certified by Dr. Richard Bandler himself, have at least received their training from the original source – and continuous developer – of NLP.

I am sure there are also other quite capable and knowledgeable NLP practitioners, but, due to what has been said above, I feel that a certificate issued by Richard Bandler is by far the best and most reliable proof of NLP skills and knowledge. It is, however, good to remember that a mere certificate or license does not make a person professional. Certificates or licenses are only pieces of evidence that the person in question has received the appropriate training. Only by bringing the learned skills to practice and by continuously updating and developing their skills and knowledge will prove their know-how.

Since there are all kinds of so called "NLP practitioners," I recommend that you make sure that your NLP Coach or NLP Trainer is licensed by the developer, Dr. Richard Bandler, himself. Also remember that only working with the Coach will then conclusively prove whether your choice has been a right one.

Resources for the Quotes

Richard Bandler: Get the Life You Want

Richard Bandler: Guide to Trance-formation

Richard Bandler & John LaValle: Persuasion Engineering

Richard Bandler & Garner Thomson: The Secrets of Being Happy

Shelle Rose Charvet: Words That Change Minds

Deepak Chopra: The Seven Spiritual Laws of Success

Terttu Grönfors & Trygve Roos: Mitä on NLP

Bill Harris: Thresholds of the Mind

Napoleon Hill: Think and Grow Rich

Paul McKenna: Change Your Life in Seven Days

Anders Piper: Shortcut to Flow

Bob Proctor: You Were Born Rich

Anthony Robbins: Unlimited Power

Bobbe Sommer: Psycho Cybernetics 2000

About the Author

Hannu Pirilä is the CEO and founder of HPA Consulting, as well as a Coach and the Head Trainer at Flow Mentaalivalmennus (Flow Mental Coaching), which he co-founded with Timo Räkköläinen, the owner and Head Teacher of Helsinki Self-Defense School Ltd (Hipko).

Hannu has eMBA (executive Master of Business Administration) and BSc decrees and he is an Accredited Associate and Business Adviser of the IIB (Institute for Independent Business International) and Member of the Board at LAK ry (Business Management Advisory Services). Hannu is also a Licensed Master Practitioner and Trainer of NLP®, Licensed NLP Coach™, Licensed Sports Performance Coach™, Licensed Master Business Practitioner of NLP™, Specialist Practitioner of Neuro-Hypnotic Repatterning™, Licensed LAB Profile™ Practitioner and Clinical Hypnotherapist.

Hannu works as a Business Consultant and Business Coach, as well as an NLP Trainer, NLP Coach, a speaker in seminars and other events and as a Mental Sports Coach. In business world, Hannu has consulted both entrepreneurs and publicly listed corporations. In the world of sports, Hannu has acted as a mental coach for junior basketball teams as well as professional soccer players, for amateur tennis players as well as for an MMA World Champion. In addition to the above, Hannu has, among other things, helped a number of people with things like getting rid of a fear and phobias, stop smoking, lose weight, and to make other remarkable changes to improve the qualities of their lives. In short, Hannu is one of the leading Personal Development and NLP Coaches in Finland.

Hannu has studied under the world-famous masters of personal development, like Dr. Richard Bandler, John LaValle, Bill Harris and Bob Proctor. Hannu also regularly serves as a team member of Assistant Trainers at the seminars of the developer of NLP, Dr. Richard Bandler, in Orlando, USA, and London, England.

Hannu's mission is to help people and companies to achieve mental well-being and success.

For more information on Hannu and his services, please visit:

www.hannupirila.com